redefining
life: **MYIDENTITY**

redefining life: MYIDENTITY

A NAVSTUDY FEATURING THE**MESSAGE**®//REMIX™

Written and compiled by Margaret Feinberg

Th1nk Books
an imprint of NavPress®

TH1NK
P.O. Box 35001
Colorado Springs, Colorado 80935

TH1NK is an imprint of NavPress.
TH1NK and the TH1NK logo are registered trademarks of NavPress. Absence of ® in connection with marks of NavPress or other parties does not indicate an absence of registration of those marks.

ISBN 1-57683-828-5

Cover design by Kirk DouPonce, Dog Eared Design
Cover photo by Digital Vision
Creative Team: Gabe Filkey, s.c.m., Steve Parolini, Arvid Wallen, Amy Spencer,
        Kathy Mosier, Glynese Northam

Written and compiled by Margaret Feinberg

Some of the anecdotal illustrations in this book are true to life and are included with the permission of the persons involved. All other illustrations are composites of real situations, and any resemblance to people living or dead is coincidental.

Printed in Canada

1 2 3 4 5 6 7 8 9 10 / 09 08 07 06 05

contents

about the redefininglife series

It's in Christ that we find out who we are and what we are living for.

Ephesians 1:11

For most of your life, you've been a student. And yet in a moment—probably marked by a ceremony—the title you carried for more than a dozen years was stripped away. So now how will you describe yourself when people ask? Are you a professional? An adult? A temporarily unemployed graduate? What seems to fit? Or do any of these fit at all?

Expectations are probably pretty high. But only a few of your graduating class fall into the life you wish you could have—the great job, the wonderful lifelong relationship, the incredible devotion to God. For the rest of you, it's back to square one in many ways. What has been defined for you in the past is suddenly up for negotiation.

The discussion guides in the REDEFINING LIFE series give you a forum to help with that negotiation process. They can help you figure out who you are, *who you really are*, whether you're still taking classes, employed full-time, or somewhere in between. They can help you find out what's really important in life; how to thrive in your work; and how to grow lifelong, meaningful relationships.

REDEFINING LIFE is a place to ask the hard questions of yourself and others. We're talking about a "marrow deep" kind of honesty. At the very least, these discussion guides will show you that you're not alone in the process of self-definition. And hopefully, they will also give you a glimpse—or maybe more—of God's role in the defining of you.

introduction

At about the same time, the disciples came to
Jesus asking, "Who gets the highest rank in God's
kingdom?" For an answer Jesus called over a child,
whom he stood in the middle of the room, and said,
"I'm telling you, once and for all, that unless
you return to square one and start over like
children, you're not even going to get a look at
the kingdom, let alone get in. Whoever becomes
simple and elemental again, like this child, will
rank high in God's kingdom. What's more, when you
receive the childlike on my account, it's the same
as receiving me."

Matthew 18:1-5

Who are you? Who are you when no one is watching? Who are you when no
one is listening? Who are you when it's just you alone in a room with God?
Who are you, really?

These are tough questions—the kind that cut to the core of our being.
They strip us of our titles, our background, our ethnicity, our family name,
and our possessions (or lack thereof). These questions reduce us to the least
common denominator—simply being human, without all the pomp and cir-
cumstance that the world tries to dress us in. And in that moment we become
childlike and enter into what Christ calls "simple and elemental" so we can get
a better look at what He intended us to become all along.

So who are you? Only you can know. And part of the journey of self-discovery
is God-discovery because He's the One who fashioned you.

Why bother? Why poke and prod in such uncomfortable places? Because
there is freedom in knowing who you are. In the process, you not only discover
what you were created for, but also learn about the One who created you. Then,
when you're faced with redefining what you're going to do with your life and

where you're supposed to go and who you'll be, you will have what others don't: solid ground to stand on. When the storms come and the winds blow—and they will—you'll be anchored.

how to use this discussion guide

REDEFINING LIFE isn't like any other study. We're not kidding. REDEFINING LIFE isn't designed with easy, obvious-to-answer questions and nice fill-in-the-blanks. It's got more of a wide-open-spaces feel to it.

The process is simple, really. Complete a lesson *on your own* (see details below). Then get with your small group and go through it again *together*. Got it?

Okay, want a little more direction than that? Here you go. And if you want even more help, check out the Discussion Group Study Tips (page 133) and the Frequently Asked Questions (page 135) sections in the back of the book.

1. Read, read, read. Each lesson contains five sections, but don't think of them as homework. This isn't an assignment to be graded. And at the end of the week, you don't have to turn it in to a teacher, professor, or boss. So don't read this as a "have to" but as a "get to." Think about how you read when you're on vacation. Set a leisurely pace. Try to enjoy what you read. Then read it again. Allow the words and meaning to soak in. Use the First Thoughts box to record

first thoughts
like:
dislike:
agree:
disagree:
don't get it:

your initial reactions to the text. (That's a sample on the previous page.) Then use the space provided in and around the reading to make notes. What bugs you? What inspires you? What doesn't make sense? What's confusing? Be honest. Be real. Be yourself. Don't shy away from phrases or sentences you don't understand or don't like. Circle them. Cross them out. Add exclamation marks or smiley faces.

2. Think about what you read. Think about what you wrote. Always ask:

- What does this mean?
- Why does this matter?
- How does this relate to my life right now?
- What does Scripture have to say about this?

Then respond to the questions provided. If you have a knack for asking questions, don't be shy about writing some of your own. You may have a lot to say on one topic, little on another. That's okay. When you come back to the passages in your small group, listen. Allow the experience of others to broaden your understanding and wisdom. You'll be stretched here — called on to evaluate what you've discovered and asked to make practical sense of it. In community, that stretching can often be painful and sometimes even embarrassing. But your willingness to be transparent — your openness to the possibility of personal growth — will reap great rewards. Vulnerability spurs growth in yourself and others.

3. Pray as you go through the entire session — before you begin reading, as you're thinking about a passage and its questions, and especially before you get together in a small group. Pause 'n' pray whenever you need to ask God for help along the way. Prayer takes many forms. You can speak your prayers. Be silent. Write them in the space at the bottom of each page. You can pray a Scripture or a spiritual song. Just don't forget that one of the most important parts of prayer is taking time to listen for God's response.

4. Live. What good are study, reflection, and prayer if they don't lead to action? When reflecting on the week's worth of lessons, think about what impacted you and how you can turn that lesson into action. After studying the issue of forgiveness, you may realize you need to write a letter or an email to someone. After studying God's generosity, you may feel compelled to give a gift to a particular outreach. Figure out what God is calling you to do to live out your faith. Sometimes you'll finish a week's worth of lessons and each group member will decide to commit to the same goal. Other times you'll each walk away with a different conviction or goal. Record your goals in the book.

5. Follow up. What good are information and conversation if they don't lead to transformation? Your goal in doing any good study is to ultimately become more like Christ, and this is no exception. Prepare yourself to take your faith and make it active and alive. Be willing to set goals and hold others (as well as be held) accountable in your group. Part of being in a community of Jesus-followers means asking, "Hey, did you do what you said you were going to do?" It will help you put your faith into action as part of a community.

6. Repeat as necessary.

uncovering
your
true self

We don't yet see things clearly. We're squinting in a fog, peering through a mist. But it won't be long before the weather clears and the sun shines bright! We'll see it all then, see it all as clearly as God sees us, knowing him directly just as he knows us!

1 Corinthians 13:12

the defining line

We start every lesson by asking you to do a sometimes-difficult thing: define the core truths about the study topic as it relates to you right now. Use this "beginning place" to set the foundation for the lesson. You can then build, change, adjust, and otherwise redefine your life from there.

If you had to introduce yourself to a group in a hundred words or less, what would you say? Think about the things you would share. What would you mention? Your history. Your background. Your family. Your job. Record your introduction in the space below before reading any further.

Now, think a little deeper about who you are for a moment. Everything you've just written offers insightful pieces of information about you, but it's only the tip of the iceberg. Let's get beyond the obvious labels of job titles and heritage and press a little deeper. If you had to tell someone who you are—without mentioning your history, background, family, or job, what would you say? How would you describe yourself? What hidden thoughts, dreams, memories, hopes, and passions would you share? Which ones would you choose to hold back? Use the space below to describe the real you.

Consider sharing one or both of the descriptions with your discussion group when you meet.

read Could You Turn the Stereo(type) Down?

From "A Clear and Present Identity" by Frederica Matthewes-Green[1]

I'm trying to remember a man I once knew. What was his name again? It was one of those Swiss names. If you draw a blank at the concept of "one of those Swiss names," you're typical. Some nationalities bring to mind richly detailed associations, and Swiss is not one of them. Rummaging in the corners of memory, we might come up with a dated impression of chocolate, cuckoo clocks, neutrality, and Heidi. Wait a minute, forget Heidi—she was Austrian.

We live in an age that encourages a high degree of self-consciousness about identity, and some identities are more fully costumed than others. Head south into Italy and you immediately find a complete and colorful package, so generally appealing that Italian-Americans sport bumper stickers that read "Kiss Me, I'm Italian" ("Kiss Me, I'm Norwegian" is not as popular). Every Italian, as we well know, is exuberant, warm-hearted, and a great cook. Even Mafia associations become, in pop entertainment, colorful and harmless. If people could sign up for the ethnic stereotype they most wanted to portray, the list of voluntary Italians would be long.

Go not much farther south and encounter Arabs, who are assigned Italians' volatile temperament but not their sweetening charm. In the public imagination, they are "dirty Arabs," unreasonable and fanatical, and potentially violent. When *Back to the Future* wanted bad guys to covet the professor's plutonium, it gave Arabs the role. Among North Americans, the line to sign up to portray Arabs would not be long.

The question of identity is significant for Christians because we are each on a lifelong journey to find out who we really are. We are like miners trapped at the bottom of a caved-in shaft trying to tunnel through debris to the light. Jesus calls us toward Himself, but sins and selfishness impede us. Our natural state is one of confusion. Prone to self-deception, we don't readily know which elements of self to value and which to deplore. Examination of conscience is a lost art.

---

first thoughts

like:

dislike:

agree:

disagree:

don't get it:

---

think

- If you could choose a stereotype for yourself, which one would you choose? Why? What do you think that says about you?
- To what degree do you think stereotypes are true? To what degree do they uncover a person's identity? To what degree do they hide a person's identity?
- Why do you think the issue of identity is significant? Do you agree with Matthews-Greene's observation that "we are each on a lifelong journey to find out who we really are"? Why or why not?
- Respond to this quote: "Examination of conscience is a lost art."

pray

read What Does True Identity Look Like?

1 Corinthians 5:1-8

I also received a report of scandalous sex within your church family, a kind that wouldn't be tolerated even outside the church: One of your men is sleeping with his stepmother. And you're so above it all that it doesn't even faze you! Shouldn't this break your hearts? Shouldn't it bring you to your knees in tears? Shouldn't this person and his conduct be confronted and dealt with?

I'll tell you what I would do. Even though I'm not there in person, consider me right there with you, because I can fully see what's going on. I'm telling you that this is wrong. You must not simply look the other way and hope it goes away on its own. Bring it out in the open and deal with it in the authority of Jesus our Master. Assemble the community—I'll be present in spirit with you and our Master Jesus will be present in power. Hold this man's conduct up to public scrutiny. Let him defend it if he can! But if he can't, then out with him! It will be totally devastating to him, of course, and embarrassing to you. But better devastation and embarrassment than damnation. You want him on his feet and forgiven before the Master on the Day of Judgment.

Your flip and callous arrogance in these things bothers me. You pass it off as a small thing, but it's anything but that. Yeast, too, is a "small thing," but it works its way through a whole batch of bread dough pretty fast. So get rid of this "yeast." Our true identity is flat and plain, not puffed up with the wrong kind of ingredient. The Messiah, our Passover Lamb, has already been sacrificed for the Passover meal, and we are the Unraised Bread part of the Feast. So let's live out our part in the Feast, not as raised bread swollen with the yeast of evil, but as flat bread—simple, genuine, unpretentious.

first thoughts

like:

dislike:

agree:

disagree:

don't get it:

think

- What words does Paul use to describe our authentic identity? How do those words compare to what we hear from friends? Coworkers? Employers? Television, movies, and other media?
- In what ways would you describe yourself as raised bread? In what ways would you describe yourself as flat bread?
- Why kinds of "yeast" have you allowed in your own life?
- What does it take to become the "flat bread" Paul describes? How can *you* do this? Do you even want to?

pray

read Who You Are Without the Fanfare

From "Take Five with Kurt Warner," an article in *Today's Christian Woman*[2]

Super Bowl champion and [former] St. Louis Rams quarterback Kurt Warner hasn't always had a glamorous life. Drafted and then cut from the NFL in 1994, Kurt supported himself by stocking shelves at a local grocery store. After his supermarket days, Kurt played arena football and in the NFL Europe, where he fully committed his life to Christ.

With all the publicity, does ego ever become a problem? When I was cut from the NFL and worked in a grocery store to make ends meet, I learned about finding my identity in Christ. That's helped me remember everything I have is a gift from God.

How do you continually keep your standards high? We have a group of guys on the team who are believers. We regularly meet for Bible study, accountability, and prayer before games. We hope to show some of the younger guys on the team who are seeking "religion" that Christ's available to them, too.

I also make sure my family gets to church weekly. These things remind me no matter what I do, if I make mistakes or fumble things in life, God's always there for me.

---

first thoughts

like:

dislike:

agree:

disagree:

don't get it:

---

think

- What did hard times teach Kurt Warner about his identity? What have hard times taught you about your genuine identity?
- Which has taught you more about yourself: times of ease, or times of difficulty? Why?
- Think of one particularly difficult time in your life. What did you learn about yourself by going through it?
- What does the presence and makeup of your community — friends, family members, and coworkers — reveal about you? Why are other people so important to figuring out who you really are?

pray

read Stripped of the Glitz and Glamour

Madonna, as quoted in *Vanity Fair*[3]

All my will has always been to conquer some horrible feeling of inadequacy. I'm always struggling with that fear. I push past one spell of it and discover myself as a special human being, and then I get to another stage and I think I'm mediocre and uninteresting. And I find a way to get myself out of that. Again and again. My drive in life is from this horrible fear of being mediocre. And that's always pushing me, pushing me. Because even though I've become Somebody, I still have to prove that I'm Somebody. My struggle has never ended, and it probably never will.

first thoughts

like:

dislike:

agree:

disagree:

don't get it:

think

- Are you surprised by Madonna's insecurities? Why or why not? In what ways do you relate to them?
- Reread the paragraph. How does Madonna's vulnerability make you feel about her? Do you feel like you understand her any better? Does it affect the way you think about her?
- When you look at your own life, what fears and insecurities drive you to do the things you do?
- If you were willing to share those fears and insecurities with the other members of your discussion group, do you think they

would still care for you? Do you think their compassion for you would increase or decrease based on what you shared?

- What prevents you from sharing them?
- Do you expect your struggle will ever end? Why or why not?

pray

read True Identity Revealed

Genesis 45:1-28

Joseph couldn't hold himself in any longer, keeping up a front before all his attendants. He cried out, "Leave! Clear out—everyone leave!" So there was no one with Joseph when he identified himself to his brothers. But his sobbing was so violent that the Egyptians couldn't help but hear him. The news was soon reported to Pharaoh's palace.

Joseph spoke to his brothers: "I am Joseph. Is my father really still alive?" But his brothers couldn't say a word. They were speechless—they couldn't believe what they were hearing and seeing.

"Come closer to me," Joseph said to his brothers. They came closer. "I am Joseph your brother whom you sold into Egypt. But don't feel badly, don't blame yourselves for selling me. God was behind it. God sent me here ahead of you to save lives. There has been a famine in the land now for two years; the famine will continue for five more years—neither plowing nor harvesting. God sent me on ahead to pave the way and make sure there was a remnant in the land, to save your lives in an amazing act of deliverance. So you see, it wasn't you who sent me here but God. He set me in place as a father to Pharaoh, put me in charge of his personal affairs, and made me ruler of all Egypt.

"Hurry back to my father. Tell him, 'Your son Joseph says: I'm master of all of Egypt. Come as fast as you can and join me here. I'll give you a place to live in Goshen where you'll be close to me—you, your children, your grandchildren, your flocks, your herds, and anything else you can think of. I'll take care of you there completely. There are still five more years of famine ahead; I'll make sure all your needs are taken care of, you and everyone connected with you—you won't want for a thing.'

"Look at me. You can see for yourselves, and my brother Benjamin can see for himself, that it's me, my own mouth, telling you all this. Tell my father all about the high position I hold in Egypt, tell him everything you've seen here, but don't take all day—hurry up and get my father down here."

Then Joseph threw himself on his brother Benjamin's neck and wept, and Benjamin wept on his neck. He then kissed all his brothers and wept over them. Only then were his brothers able to talk with him.

The story was reported in Pharaoh's palace: "Joseph's brothers have come." It was good news to Pharaoh and all who worked with him.

Pharaoh said to Joseph, "Tell your brothers, 'This is the plan: Load up your pack animals; go to Canaan, get your father and your families and bring them back here. I'll settle you on the best land in Egypt—you'll live off the fat of the land.'

"Also tell them this: 'Here's what I want you to do: Take wagons from Egypt to carry your little ones and your wives and load up your father and come back. Don't worry about having to leave things behind; the best in all of Egypt will be yours.'"

And they did just that, the sons of Israel. Joseph gave them the wagons that Pharaoh had promised and food for the trip. He outfitted all the brothers in brand-new clothes, but he gave Benjamin three hundred pieces of silver and several suits of clothes. He sent his father these gifts: ten donkeys loaded with Egypt's best products and another ten donkeys loaded with grain and bread, provisions for his father's journey back.

Then he sent his brothers off. As they left he told them, "Take it easy on the journey; try to get along with each other."

They left Egypt and went back to their father Jacob in Canaan. When they told him, "Joseph is still alive—and he's the ruler over the whole land of Egypt!" he went numb; he couldn't believe his ears. But the more they talked, telling him everything that Joseph had told them and when he saw the wagons that Joseph had sent to carry him back, the blood started to flow again—their father Jacob's spirit revived. Israel said, "I've heard enough—my son Joseph is still alive. I've got to go and see him before I die."

first thoughts

like:

dislike:

agree:

disagree:

don't get it:

think

- Read Genesis 43 and 44. Why was it so important for Joseph to reveal his identity?
- What prompted him to keep his identity secret for so long? How difficult was it for him to keep the secret? How did Joseph feel when he revealed the truth?
- What kind of burden do you carry when you try to be someone other than yourself?
- What situations, circumstances, or people tempt you to be someone other than your true self? How can you resist the temptation?

pray

live   The Redefining

Take a few moments to skim through the notes you've made in these readings. What do they tell you about how you see "your true self"? Based on what you've read and discussed, is there anything you want to change? Describe this below.

What, if anything, is stopping you from making this change?

What can you do in the upcoming month to get to know yourself better? What do you want to say to God (or ask of Him) about this?

Are there things about yourself that you just don't like? Are you ever tempted to hide from yourself? What can you do over the next week to get really honest with yourself? What steps can you take to see yourself as Christ sees you — even in those areas?

Talk with a close friend about all of the above. Brainstorm together about what it might take to move toward God in this area of your life. Determine what this looks like in a practical sense and then list any measurable goals you want to shoot for here. Review these goals each week to see how you're doing.

that which never changes

Now that we know what we have—Jesus, this great High Priest with ready access to God—let's not let it slip through our fingers. We don't have a priest who is out of touch with our reality. He's been through weakness and testing, experienced it all—all but the sin. So let's walk right up to him and get what he is so ready to give. Take the mercy, accept the help.

Hebrews 4:14-16

a reminder

Before you dive into this study, spend a little time reviewing what you wrote in the previous lesson's Live section. How are you doing? Check with your small-group members and review your progress toward the specified goals. If necessary, adjust your goals and plans and then recommit to them.

the defining line

We live in a world of constant change. Things are in continuous motion around us—people, circumstances, trials, and triumphs. And there is invariable motion *within* us as we wrestle with what it means to live life in the context of our faith.

Yet even while you move through a world of continuous change, some things remain the same. Some things you enjoy and value today you'll *always* enjoy and value—no matter what happens. And some things you dislike and avoid today you will always dislike and avoid. Just for fun, list a few of these things you expect won't change (or perhaps *hope* won't change).

If you go a little deeper, you may find there are core truths about you that never change as well. When you want to get back to the roots of who you really are, where do you go? What do you do? What do you reflect on? What are these core truths? Record your responses below.

Consider sharing some of these thoughts with your discussion group.

read What's in a Name?

Luke 1:57-66

When Elizabeth was full-term in her pregnancy, she bore a son. Her neighbors and relatives, seeing that God had overwhelmed her with mercy, celebrated with her.

On the eighth day, they came to circumcise the child and were calling him Zachariah after his father. But his mother intervened: "No. He is to be called John."

"But," they said, "no one in your family is named that." They used sign language to ask Zachariah what he wanted him named.

Asking for a tablet, Zachariah wrote, "His name is to be John." That took everyone by surprise. Surprise followed surprise—Zachariah's mouth was now open, his tongue loose, and he was talking, praising God!

A deep, reverential fear settled over the neighborhood, and in all that Judean hill country people talked about nothing else. Everyone who heard about it took it to heart, wondering, "What will become of this child? Clearly, God has his hand in this."

---

first thoughts

like:

dislike:

agree:

disagree:

don't get it:

---

think

- What is the story behind how your name was chosen? Is there anyone you were named after? What do you know about that person?
- Perhaps you know the meaning of your name. Does the meaning match who you are? What meaning would you attribute to your name that would best match you?
- What things in your life suggest that God has a specific idea about who He has created you to be?
- What things in your life make you wonder *if* God has a specific idea about who He has created you to be?
- How do you reconcile your answers to the two previous questions?

pray

read Still Who We Are

From *People* magazine[1]

One terrible day in 1984, surgeons told Angilee Wallis her son Terry was lost to her forever. The 20-year-old had crashed through a guardrail in a pickup truck and plunged off a lonely Ozark mountain road. Paralyzed from the neck down, he was in a vegetative state, walled off from loved ones, including an infant daughter. "One doctor told us, 'This isn't TV,'" Angilee recalls. "He said, 'People in comas don't just come out of it and everything's fine.'"

Still, for the next 19 years, Angilee, 55, hoped for a miracle, visiting her son twice a week at a rehab center near the family ranch in rural Round Mountain, Ark., to talk to him and hold his hand. But although Terry, now 39, could swallow food and open his eyes, he never uttered a word. That is, until June 11, when his mother showed up to see him and a nurse asked him who the visitor was. "Mom," he replied. Says Angilee: "I nearly fell over, Terry was grinning. I ran to him and hugged him, I said, 'Say it again!'"

He has—and more. Within five days of his awakening, Terry had begun speaking simple sentences. Seeing his daughter, Amber, now 19 and married, for the first time, he declared, "I love you—you're so beautiful." Regaining consciousness after so many years is so rare that no statistics are kept, but experts believe Terry may hold the record for reviving after the longest period in a vegetative state.

Asked today about the accident, Terry insists he never had one. He recognizes his parents and siblings and his memories of life before the fateful night, but cannot grasp all that has happened since. The extent of permanent brain damage he has suffered is still unknown. "Sometimes he says, 'You're my baby girl,' and sometimes he doesn't seem to

first thoughts

like:

dislike:

agree:

disagree:

don't get it:

know me," says Amber. Adds Angilee: "He doesn't really ask about anything." He did want to check out her cell phone though. "He asked me to call his grandmother," she says, "and rattled off her number from 1984."

think

- If you just awoke from five or ten years in a coma, what do you think your personality would be like? How would it be different from who you really are today?
- What about your personality today makes you glad you were not "frozen in time" for the past five or ten years? What about your personality today makes you wish you *were* frozen in time?
- Is it possible to become a completely different person over time? What aspects of "who you are" come from your experiences?
- Is your relationship with God molding you into a different person? Should it? Explain.

pray

read Who You Are in Christ

1 Corinthians 12:27

You are Christ's body—that's who you are! You must never forget this. Only as you accept your part of that body does your "part" mean anything.

John 1:12

But whoever did want him,
    who believed he was who he claimed
    and would do what he said,
He made to be their true selves,
    their child-of-God selves.

John 15:15

I'm no longer calling you servants because servants don't understand what their master is thinking and planning. No, I've named you friends because I've let you in on everything I've heard from the Father.

2 Corinthians 1:21-22

God affirms us, making us a sure thing in Christ, putting his Yes within us. By his Spirit he has stamped us with his eternal pledge—a sure beginning of what he is destined to complete.

---

first thoughts

like:

dislike:

agree:

disagree:

don't get it:

---

think

- What do these Scriptures say about who you are in Christ? Circle the key phrases and words that are used in each passage to describe you. Do any of them surprise you?
- Are any of the phrases or words going to change as you continue your walk with Christ? What are the unchanging truths about you?
- How much of your identity is found in what God has created you to *be?* How much of your identity is found in what God has created you to *do?*

pray

read Finding Identity Amid the Noise

From "The Decline and Fall of Personality" by Kenneth J. Gergen[2]

We are exposed to more opinions, values, personalities, and ways of life than was any previous generation in history; the number of our relationships soars, the variations are enormous: past relationships remain (only a phone call apart) and new faces are only a channel away. There is, in short, an explosion in social connection.

What does this explosion have to do with our sense of selves, who we are, and what we stand for? How does it undermine beliefs in a romantic interior or in a rational center of the self?

First, there is a populating of the self, that is, an absorption of others into ourselves. Through countless exposure to others, we rapidly increase the range of appreciations, understandings, and action possibilities available to us. . . .

The sense of a centered self also begins to collapse under the demands of multiple audiences. In one of the most rousing scenes from the film *Bugsy*, the infamous gangster (played by Warren Beatty) races desperately from one room of his mansion to another. Breathlessly he plays the affable host for his daughter's birthday party, abandons her to plead for the affection of his doubting wife, reappears with swagger and gusto to impress his gangster cronies in the adjoining room, only to race away again to his daughter's failing party. As we laugh, pity, and loathe this poor figure, we are simultaneously reacting to our own lives. For the socializing technologies are constructing an enormous mansion of conflicting demands for each one of us.

first thoughts

like:

dislike:

agree:

disagree:

don't get it:

think

- In what ways have you experienced the "explosion in social connection"? How do you think that has impacted your identity?
- Do you think you "absorb" others into yourself? What impact does that have on how you define yourself?
- How has your identity responded to the "demands of multiple audiences"?
- In what ways are you shaped by the absorption of others and the demands of multiple audiences? How does your core identity in Christ fit in all of this?

pray

read Fully Known

Romans 8:26-28

Meanwhile, the moment we get tired in the waiting, God's Spirit is right alongside helping us along. If we don't know how or what to pray, it doesn't matter. He does our praying in and for us, making prayer out of our wordless sighs, our aching groans. He knows us far better than we know ourselves, knows our pregnant condition, and keeps us present before God. That's why we can be so sure that every detail in our lives of love for God is worked into something good.

Ephesians 2:10

No, we neither make nor save ourselves. God does both the making and saving. He creates each of us by Christ Jesus to join him in the work he does, the good work he has gotten ready for us to do, work we had better be doing.

1 Corinthians 12:27

You are Christ's body—that's who you are! You must never forget this. Only as you accept your part of that body does your "part" mean anything.

---

first thoughts

like:

dislike:

agree:

disagree:

don't get it:

---

think

- How does God hear your heart when you can't find the words?
- In what way is this a core truth of your identity in Christ?
- What does it feel like to be known this intimately? How do you naturally respond to intimacy?
- How does knowing yourself enable you to be a more active member of the body of Christ?

pray

live   The Redefining

Take a few moments to skim through the notes you've made in these readings. What do they tell you about your identity? Based on what you've read and discussed, is there anything you want to change? Describe this below.

What, if anything, is stopping you from making this change?

Are you allowing anyone or anything to define who you really are and what you really believe? If so, who or what is defining you? What are the results of that in your life? Do you need to make a change?

In what ways do you see your identity in Christ being lived out in real time? In what areas of your life are you living as the world defines you? Take some time this week to write a summary below of who you really are in Christ. Post this somewhere you'll see it regularly.

Talk with a close friend about all of the above. Brainstorm together about what it might take to move toward God in this area of your life. Determine what this looks like in a practical sense and then list any measurable goals you want to shoot for here. Review these goals each week to see how you're doing.

what makes you?

"In a word, what I'm saying is, *Grow up.* You're kingdom subjects. Now live like it. Live out your God-created identity. Live generously and graciously toward others, the way God lives toward you."

Matthew 5:48

a reminder

Before you dive into this study, spend a little time reviewing what you wrote in the previous lessons' Live sections. How are you doing? Check with your small-group members and review your progress toward the specified goals. If necessary, adjust your goals and plans and then recommit to them.

the defining line

God knows your name. God knows your background, history, and foundation. He knows your quirks and your qualms, your hopes and your dreams, your failures and your misgivings. God knows the innermost fabric of your being—your soul, spirit, mind—all of it. He knows it all. But how much do you know about yourself? When was the last time you reflected on who you really are? Use the space below to record things that make you *you.*

Think about the list you made. How do these reflect your relationship with God? Share some of these "beginning thoughts" with your small group if you feel comfortable doing so.

read From the Beginning

Romans 8:29-30

God knew what he was doing from the very beginning. He decided from the outset to shape the lives of those who love him along the same lines as the life of his Son. The Son stands first in the line of humanity he restored. We see the original and intended shape of our lives there in him. After God made that decision of what his children should be like, he followed it up by calling people by name. After he called them by name, he set them on a solid basis with himself. And then, after getting them established, he stayed with them to the end, gloriously completing what he had begun.

---

first thoughts

like:

dislike:

agree:

disagree:

don't get it:

---

think

- Does knowing God's eternal design comfort you about the future? Why or why not?
- If you had to pick a shape to describe your life, what would you choose? (Draw it if you'd like.) Why does this describe you?

- What would a God-designed shape look like? What changes do you need to make to restore the God-designed shape for your life?
- Describe the specific ways in which God is reshaping your life right now.

pray

read Who Is Creating You Today?

From "Who I'm Not" by Caleb C. Anderson[1]

I believe in a Creator God. That makes me a created being. If He's God and I'm His creation, things immediately stop being up to me because they never were.

But we are so confused in this country about who God is—that's ultimately why we don't know who we are. Am I God? Who's been calling the shots in your life today? Is culture God? Who are you appealing to? Are they God? Who are you trying to please?

We can't talk about the effects of culture on our personal lives without talking about rampant insecurity. We can't talk about insecurity without talking about true identity. We can't talk about true identity without talking about a Creative God . . . the God who created you.

But who's creating you today? Are you trying to reinvent yourself? Still haven't found yourself? Our culture is constructed to keep us in the perpetual hunt, but we can stop now. There's nowhere else to look.

Men, it's not on the Internet. Women, it's not in stores. No doctor has the prescription to insecurity. No psychic can tell you who you were created to be. In our culture of choices, choose you —stripped, scarred, bruised, and seemingly alone. That's a formula for God's transforming presence. In choosing you—the rough, raw, original you—you are choosing to live for God, the only truly Authentic One.

first thoughts
like:
dislike:
agree:
disagree:
don't get it:

think

- In what ways do you think of yourself as a god?
- How does the presence of a true God remind you of your true self?
- How well do you really know yourself? What prevents you from knowing yourself better?
- In your experience, when are the most tender times for God to influence your true identity?

pray

read A Divine Creation

Psalm 139:13-16

I thank you, High God — you're breathtaking!
> Body and soul, I am marvelously made!
> I worship in adoration — what a creation!
You know me inside and out,
> you know every bone in my body;
You know exactly how I was made, bit by bit,
> how I was sculpted from nothing into something.
Like an open book, you watched me grow from conception to birth;
> all the stages of my life were spread out before you,
The days of my life all prepared
> before I'd even lived one day.

---

first thoughts

like:

dislike:

agree:

disagree:

don't get it:

---

think

- What does this passage say about God's love for you? What about this passage is encouragement for you? What about it bothers you or makes you question God?
- Is there such a thing as privacy from God? Explain.
- What are the advantages of a God who doesn't respect our privacy? What are the disadvantages?
- How often do you feel that the days of your life were prepared before you were born? How does that affect how you view the struggles you face this week?

pray

read Made in Heaven

Psalm 100

On your feet now—applaud GOD!
    Bring a gift of laughter,
    sing yourselves into his presence.

Know this: GOD is God, and God, GOD.
    He made us; we didn't make him.
    We're his people, his well-tended sheep.

Enter with the password: "Thank you!"
    Make yourselves at home, talking praise.
    Thank him. Worship him.

For GOD is sheer beauty,
    all-generous in love,
    loyal always and ever.

---

first thoughts

like:

dislike:

agree:

disagree:

don't get it:

---

think

- When you close your eyes and try to picture God, what does He look like?
- If a creation reflects its creator, how do you reflect God?
- Does knowing God as your Creator affect your relationship with Him? Explain.
- How much do you identify with God? How is your identity affected by God?

pray

read A Secret Identity

John Mackey, CEO, Whole Foods Market[2]

My trail name is Strider. . . . I'm a great admirer of Tolkien's *Lord of the Rings*. . . . Before I was in high school, I had read it five times. And one of the characters I admired was Strider. . . . Strider isn't his real name; it's his nickname on the trail. He is really Aragorn, the king. But he wasn't a king on the trail. In 2002 when I was hiking, I was certainly the richest guy hiking the Appalachian Trail. I was a kind of secret king. But that wasn't my identity, or my role, on the trail.

---

first thoughts

like:

dislike:

agree:

disagree:

don't get it:

---

think

- Of all the characters in *Lord of the Rings,* whom do you admire most? Of all the characters in the Bible, whom do you resonate with most? In what ways does this choice reflect your true identity?

- What does it mean that your identity is hidden in Christ?
- If you had to give yourself a secret name, what would it be? Why? What secret name might God give you? Is that different from the name you'd want God to give you? Explain.

pray

live   The Redefining

Take a few moments to skim through the notes you've made in these readings. What do they tell you about your defining characteristics? Based on what you've read and discussed, is there anything you want to change? Describe this below.

What, if anything, is stopping you from making this change?

What is shaping your life today? In what ways are you living out your identity in Christ? In what ways are you struggling with that identity?

Are there things in your life that you've held back from sharing with God? Is there anything that you think He's tired of hearing about or just can't handle? What stops you from being truly honest with Him?

Talk with a close friend about all of the above. Brainstorm together about what it might take to move toward God in this area of your life. Determine what this looks like in a practical sense and then list any measurable goals you want to shoot for here. Review these goals each week to see how you're doing.

great
expectations

Here is the great secret of success, my
Christian reader. Work with all your might,
but never trust in your work. Pray with all
your might for the blessing in God, but work
at the same time with all diligence, with all
patience, with all perseverance. Pray, then,
and work. Work and pray. And still again pray,
and then work. And so on, all the days of
your life. The result will surely be abundant
blessing. Whether you see much fruit or little
fruit, such kind of service will be blessed.

George Mueller

a reminder

Before you dive into this study, spend a little time reviewing what you wrote in the previous lessons' Live sections. How are you doing? Check with your small-group members and review your progress toward the specified goals. If necessary, adjust your goals and plans and then recommit to them.

the defining line

Expectations are one of the most powerful forces in nature. They drive us to perform, achieve, and succeed. Unmet expectations remind us of our weaknesses, failures, and misfortune. Left unchecked, they leave a bitter aftermath of disappointment, grief, and anger at God.

Make a list below of the healthy expectations you have for yourself.

Make a list below of unhealthy or unreasonable expectations you have for yourself. What do these say about who you really are—about your authentic identity?

read The Great Surprise

Romans 11:28-29

From your point of view as you hear and embrace the good news of the
Message, it looks like the Jews are God's enemies. But looked at from the
long-range perspective of God's overall purpose, they remain God's oldest
friends. God's gifts and God's call are under full warranty—never canceled,
never rescinded.

---

first thoughts

like:

dislike:

agree:

disagree:

don't get it:

---

think

- Describe a recent situation that disappointed you. Where did
  you see God (or not see God) in that situation?
- Have you ever encountered a situation that initially
  disappointed you, but eventually turned out to be a blessing in
  disguise? Describe.
- How has God personally revealed to you that His ways are
  higher than your ways?

- List the advantages of God's long-range perspective. What are the disadvantages? What role does God's long-range perspective play in how you define yourself?

pray

read Unexpected

From the film *The Shawshank Redemption*[1]

"My wife used to say I'm a hard man to know. Like a closed book. Complained about it all the time. She was beautiful. God, I loved her. I just didn't know how to show it, that's all. I killed her, Red; I didn't pull the trigger, but I drove her away. And that's why she died. Because of me, who I am. . . .

"I didn't [pull the trigger]; someone else did. And I wound up in here [prison]. Bad luck, I guess. It floats around; gotta land on somebody. It was my turn, that's all. I was in the path of the tornado. I just didn't expect this storm would last as long as it has.

"I know where I'd go [if I got out of prison]. Zihuatanejo. It's in Mexico. A little place on the Pacific Ocean. Know what the Mexicans say about the Pacific? It has no memory. That's where I want to live the rest of my life. A warm place with no memory. Open up a little hotel right on the beach; buy some worthless old boat and fix it up new; take my guests out charter fishing.

"I didn't shoot my wife and I didn't shoot her lover. Whatever mistakes I've made I've paid for them and then some. That hotel, that boat? I don't think that's too much to ask. [But Mexico] is down there and I'm in here.

"I guess it comes down to a simple choice, really: get busy living or get busy dying."

---

first thoughts

like:

dislike:

agree:

disagree:

don't get it:

think

- Respond to this quote: "Get busy living or get busy dying." What does your response to this say about your identity?
- How does your patience level affect your response to unmet expectations?
- What do you keep telling yourself when you have to weather a storm?
- What is your natural reaction to dashed expectations?

pray

read Expectations of a Big God

Psalm 36:5-6

God's love is meteoric,
  his loyalty astronomic,
His purpose titanic,
  his verdicts oceanic.
Yet in his largeness
  nothing gets lost;
Not a man, not a mouse,
  slips through the cracks.

---

first thoughts

like:

dislike:

agree:

disagree:

don't get it:

---

think

- Does the bigness of God vary in your mind from day to day or week to week? If so, what makes it change?
- How does the knowledge of God affect your expectations of Him? Of yourself? Of situations in your life?
- What does it mean to you that "not a man, not a mouse, slips through the cracks"? Do you ever question that? Explain.

- Does knowing God's eternal attributes provide comfort for your daily trials? How?

pray

read When the Answers Provoke New Questions

From *The Hitchhiker's Guide to the Galaxy* by Douglas Adams[2]

"Seven and a half million years our race has waited for this Great and Hopefully Exciting Day!" cried the cheerleader. "The Day of the Answer!" Hurrahs burst from the ecstatic crowd.

"Never again," cried the man, "never again will we wake up in the morning and think Who am I? What is my purpose in life? Does it really, cosmically speaking, matter if I don't get up and go to work? For today we will finally learn once and for all the plain and simple answer to all these nagging little problems of Life, the Universe and Everything!" . . .

[In another room], two severely dressed men [Phouchg and Loonquawl] sat respectfully before the terminal and waited.

"Seventy-five thousand generations ago, our ancestors set this program in motion," the second man said, "and in all that time we will be the first to hear the computer speak . . . we are the ones who will hear," said Phouchg, "the answer to the great question of Life . . . !"

"The Universe . . . !" said Loonquawl.

"And Everything . . . !"

"Shhh," said Loonquawl with a slight gesture, "I think Deep Thought [the computer] is preparing to speak!"

There was a moment's expectant pause while panels slowly came to life on the front of the console. Lights flashed on and off experimentally and settled down into a businesslike pattern. A soft low hum came from the communication channel.

"Good morning," said Deep Thought at last.

"Er . . . good morning, O Deep Thought," said Loonquawl nervously, "do you have . . . er, that is . . . "

"An answer for you?" interrupted Deep Thought majestically. "Yes. I have."

The two men shivered with expectancy. Their waiting had not been in vain.

"There really is one?" breathed Phouchg.

"There really is one," confirmed Deep Thought.

"To Everything? The great Question of Life, the Universe and Everything?"

"Yes."

Both of the men had been trained for this moment, their lives had been a preparation for it, they had been selected at birth as those who would witness the answer, but even so they found themselves gasping and squirming like excited children.

"And you're ready to give it to us?" urged Loonquawl.

"I am."

"Now?"

"Now," said Deep Thought.

They both licked their dry lips.

"Though I don't think," added Deep Thought, "that you're going to like it."

"Doesn't matter!" said Phouchg. "We must know it! Now!"

"Now?" inquired Deep Thought.

"Yes! Now . . . "

"All right," said the computer, and settled into silence again. The two men fidgeted. The tension was unbearable.

"You're really not going to like it," observed Deep Thought.

"Tell us!"

"All right," said Deep Thought. "The Answer to the Great Question . . . "

"Yes . . . !"

"Of Life, the Universe and Everything . . . " said Deep Thought.

"Yes . . . !"

"Is . . . " said Deep Thought, and paused.

"Yes . . . !"

"Is . . . "

"Yes . . . ! ! ! . . . ?"

"Forty-two," said Deep Thought, with infinite majesty and calm.

It was a long time before anyone spoke . . .

"Forty-two!" yelled Loonquawl. "Is that all you've got to show for seven and a half million years' work?"

"I checked it very thoroughly," said the computer, "and that quite definitely is the answer. I think the problem, to be quite honest with you, is that you've never actually known what the question is."

---

first thoughts

like:

dislike:

agree:

disagree:

don't get it:

---

think

- How often do God's answers to your prayers surprise you?
- What do you do when God's answers to life's situations just don't make sense?
- What questions have you been asking God that haven't been answered (or have been answered in ways you don't understand)? Could it be you're asking the wrong questions? Explain.
- In what ways do God's answers to your questions shape your identity?

pray

read Beyond Expectations

Ephesians 3:7-13

This is my life work: helping people understand and respond to this Message. It came as a sheer gift to me, a real surprise, God handling all the details. When it came to presenting the Message to people who had no background in God's way, I was the least qualified of any of the available Christians. God saw to it that I was equipped, but you can be sure that it had nothing to do with my natural abilities.

And so here I am, preaching and writing about things that are way over my head, the inexhaustible riches and generosity of Christ. My task is to bring out in the open and make plain what God, who created all this in the first place, has been doing in secret and behind the scenes all along. Through Christians like yourselves gathered in churches, this extraordinary plan of God is becoming known and talked about even among the angels!

All this is proceeding along lines planned all along by God and then executed in Christ Jesus. When we trust in him, we're free to say whatever needs to be said, bold to go wherever we need to go. So don't let my present trouble on your behalf get you down. Be proud!

---

first thoughts

like:

dislike:

agree:

disagree:

don't get it:

---

think

- In what ways did God redefine Paul's identity and abilities?
- Where do you see God working on your identity or abilities? How do your expectations of God play into that?
- How does trusting God with your hopes, dreams, desires, and prayers affect how you see yourself? How others see you?
- Respond to this excerpt: "When we trust in him, we're free to say whatever needs to be said, bold to go wherever we need to go."

pray

live   The Redefining

Take a few moments to skim through the notes you've made in these readings. What do they tell you about your expectations of God? Based on what you've read and discussed, is there anything you want to change? Describe this below.

What, if anything, is stopping you from making this change?

Make a list of the five biggest disappointments you've experienced. One by one, talk each of them over with God through prayer. Share at least one with the members of your group.

How much do you allow expectations to shape your life? In what ways do expectations propel you? In what ways do they limit you? What can you do to develop and maintain healthy expectations?

Talk with a close friend about all of the above. Brainstorm together about what it might take to move toward God in this area of your life. Determine what this looks like in a practical sense and then list any measurable goals you want to shoot for here. Review these goals each week to see how you're doing.

your
passion

[Jesus] said, "That you love the Lord your God
with all your passion and prayer and muscle and
intelligence—and that you love your neighbor
as well as you do yourself."

Luke 10:27

a reminder

*Before you dive into this study, spend a little time reviewing what you
wrote in the previous lessons' Live sections. How are you doing? Check
with your small-group members and review your progress toward the
specified goals. If necessary, adjust your goals and plans and then
recommit to them.*

the defining line

What are you passionate about? What issue—when you're discussing
it—makes you feel most alive? Your passions are part of who you are. They
help reveal your identity—what drives you, motivates you, and compels you
to respond to people, situations, and causes. Passion provides the fuel to make
a difference in your own life as well as in the lives of others.

Think about your passions. What captures your attention? What grips
your heart? List below two or three of the things you're most passionate
about.

When you're meeting with your small group, make a list of the different passions represented by group members. How broad is the spectrum of issues and topics covered? How do you think these passions help link you as the body of Christ?

read More Than a Nudge

From the introduction to *Eats, Shoots & Leaves: The Zero Tolerance Approach to Punctuation* by Lynne Truss[1]

By far the oddest and most demoralizing response to my book *[Eats, Shoots & Leaves: The Zero Tolerance Approach to Punctuation]*, however, took place at a bookshop event in Piccadilly. It is a story that, if nothing else, proves the truth of that depressing old adage about taking a horse to water. I was signing copies of my book when a rather bedraggled woman came up and said, despairingly, "Oh, I'd *love* to learn about punctuation." Spotting a sure thing (you know how it is), I said with a little laugh, "Then this is the book for you, madam!" I believe my pen actually hovered above the dedication page, as I waited for her to tell me her name.

"No, I mean it," she insisted—as if I had disagreed with her. "I really would love to know how to do it. I mean, I did learn it at school, but I've forgotten it now, and it's awful. I put all my commas in the wrong place, and as for the apostrophe . . . !" I nodded, still smiling. This all seemed familiar enough. "So shall I sign it to anyone in particular?" I said. "And I'm a teacher," she went on. "And I'm quite ashamed really, not knowing about grammar and all that; so I'd love to know about punctuation, but the trouble is, there's just nowhere you can turn, is there?"

This was quite unsettling. She shrugged, defeated, and I hoped she would go away. I said again that the book really did explain many basic things about punctuation; she said again that the basic things of punctuation were exactly what nobody was ever prepared to explain to an adult person. I must admit, I started to wonder feverishly whether I was being secretly filmed by publishers of rival punctuation books who had

first thoughts

like:

dislike:

agree:

disagree:

don't get it:

set up the whole thing. I even wondered briefly: had any author in Hatchards (a bookseller established in 1797) ever hit a customer, or was I destined to be the first? Throughout the encounter, I kept smiling at her and nodding at the book, but she never took the hint. In the end, thank goodness, she slid away, leaving me to put my coat over my head and scream. . . .

It turns out there are people whom you simply cannot help, because it suits them to say, with a shrug, "Do you know, I've always wanted to know how to use an apostrophe—and oh dear, I don't know how to wash my hair either."

think

- When it comes to your interests and desires, are you more like the author in the above excerpt or the teacher? What is the difference between wanting to do something and acting on it?
- What kind of identity crisis might the teacher be experiencing in this situation? In what ways can you relate to her?
- What happens to your identity if you never act on your heart's desires or your passions?
- How much work is involved in pursuing a passion?
- When is it right to act on a passion? When is it wrong or simply impossible?

pray

read A Flash-Point Moment

Actor Kevin Spacey[2]

I can pinpoint the exact performance where it all came together. I was playing a very negative character in the play *All My Sons* in 11th grade, and the audience virtually booed me offstage. I had this strange feeling of "Wow, I just did my job; I convinced them to think what I want them to think." It was profound—it was unlike anything I had ever experienced. From that moment I knew what I was meant to do.

I believe very strongly that if you've done well in your profession your obligation is to spend about half your time sending the elevator back down—to help others fulfill themselves. I had such great fortune because people believed in me, took me under their wing, and supported my talent long before I had ever displayed any. If you nurture someone at the right place and time, who knows what they'll do. You have to try to give it back in some way because at the end of the day that's all you can do with it. It's not like you can take it with you.

---

first thoughts

like:

dislike:

agree:

disagree:

don't get it:

---

think

- Have you ever had a moment when it "all came together"? Describe that moment.
- How do you know if you're passionate about something? What is the evidence?
- Can you be passionate about something without sharing it with others? Why or why not?
- How important is success or approval for someone who is driven by passion?

pray

read A Passion for Justice

Isaiah 16:4-6

"'Give the refugees from Moab
    sanctuary with you.
Be a safe place for those on the run
    from the killing fields.'"

"When this is all over," Judah answers,
    "the tyrant toppled,
The killing at an end,
    all signs of these cruelties long gone,
A new government of love will be established
    in the venerable David tradition.
A Ruler you can depend upon
    will head this government,
A Ruler passionate for justice,
    a Ruler quick to set things right."

---

first thoughts

like:

dislike:

agree:

disagree:

don't get it:

---

think

- What character traits would define someone who is "passionate for justice"?
- How can God use a person's passions to accomplish His will?
- How important do you think it is to be passionate about your work? Your relationships? Other aspects of your everyday life?
- What does a passion-filled life look like?
- Connect the dots from how you see your identity to how you live out your passion. How are they related?

pray

read Can a Passion Find Balance?

Bill Gates, Microsoft chairman and chief software architect[3]

If I didn't love my job so much, [taking a year off] would be a lot of fun. I'll probably find some time this decade to take some months away, but I want to contribute to Longhorn [a new Windows product] and make sure that's great; I want to help solve security problems; make sure we're driving all the other breakthroughs. With the rest of the world not being so optimistic, I like this thing where I'm going to be able to prove that there are more neat things coming. So if I didn't have that, then, yeah, I'd probably do that.

first thoughts
like:
dislike:
agree:
disagree:
don't get it:

think

- Can a passion-driven person live a balanced life? Explain.
- Can a person be too passionate about something—even if it's something good?
- At what point do passions need to be tempered?
- Describe any passions that threaten to consume you. How does tempering (or not tempering) these passions affect how you view yourself?

pray

read The Downside of Passion

From "I Know Passion" by J. L. Eubanks[4]

It's a wonderful thing to experience passion. Passion and true belief in something always appear thematically throughout movies, books, and television. So often and in such a way, in fact, that I think people often start to believe it only exists in fictitious realms, never to be taken as something real—leave it between the pages, in the theater.

But I know passion. There have been many times in my life where I've been a part of something that stirred my soul, something that touched me in a way that it couldn't be ignored or quenched. One of these, and the most intense, was the love of my God; another, the love of a woman. When your faith is all but destroyed and the one you love is lost, passion turns against you. It becomes your rage and hurt and disappointment. It becomes fuel for animosity. These are the valleys.

Then comes decision time. I chose (after some self-indulgence and self-pitying), despite these losses and hurts, to move forward with my life. Standing on the edge, I found myself much like the author of Ecclesiastes. Like the final chapter of Ecclesiastes, with a last breath of desperation and willing to risk it all, I cast my hope on the God whose existence I wasn't even sure of anymore.

---

first thoughts

like:

dislike:

agree:

disagree:

don't get it:

---

think

- How well do you know passion?
- When have you been hurt by passion? What was that like?
- Have those hurts dampened your willingness to passionately pursue something? Explain.
- How can you move beyond the hurt to live passionately again?

pray

live The Redefining

Take a few moments to skim through the notes you've made in these readings. What do they tell you about your passions? Based on what you've read and discussed, is there anything you want to change? Describe this below.

What, if anything, is stopping you from making this change?

Have you felt any nudges from God recently that you've ignored? What steps can you take this week to respond to God's leading?

If you could do anything, and time and money weren't factors, what would you do with your life? Make a list of things that are standing in the way. Talk to God about your list and what He is calling you to do.

Talk with a close friend about all of the above. Brainstorm together about what it might take to move toward God in this area of your life. Determine what this looks like in a practical sense and then list any measurable goals you want to shoot for here. Review these goals each week to see how you're doing.

the
call

God hasn't invited us into a disorderly, unkempt
life but into something holy and beautiful—as
beautiful on the inside as the outside.

1 Thessalonians 4:7

a reminder

Before you dive into this study, spend a little time reviewing what you wrote in the previous lessons' Live sections. How are you doing? Check with your small-group members and review your progress toward the specified goals. If necessary, adjust your goals and plans and then recommit to them.

the defining line

1 Samuel 3:1-10

The boy Samuel was serving GOD under Eli's direction. This was at a time when the revelation of GOD was rarely heard or seen. One night Eli was sound asleep (his eyesight was very bad—he could hardly see). It was well before dawn; the sanctuary lamp was still burning. Samuel was still in bed in the Temple of GOD, where the Chest of God rested.

   Then God called out, "Samuel, Samuel!"

   Samuel answered, "Yes? I'm here." Then he ran to Eli saying, "I heard you call. Here I am."

Eli said, "I didn't call you. Go back to bed." And so he did.

God called again, "Samuel, Samuel!"

Samuel got up and went to Eli, "I heard you call. Here I am."

Again Eli said, "Son, I didn't call you. Go back to bed." (This all happened before Samuel knew God for himself. It was before the revelation of God had been given to him personally.)

God called again, "Samuel!"—the third time! Yet again Samuel got up and went to Eli, "Yes? I heard you call me. Here I am."

That's when it dawned on Eli that God was calling the boy. So Eli directed Samuel, "Go back and lie down. If the voice calls again, say, 'Speak, God. I'm your servant, ready to listen.'" Samuel returned to his bed.

Then God came and stood before him exactly as before, calling out, "Samuel! Samuel!"

Samuel answered, "Speak. I'm your servant, ready to listen."

You probably spend quite a bit of time on the phone. Placing calls. Receiving calls. What percentage of the people you call—and who call you—do you recognize without having to say a name?

Generally speaking, the better you know someone, the easier it is to recognize his or her voice. In 1 Samuel, we read of a young boy being called by God. The voice was unrecognizable. Yet with the help of an older, wiser man, Samuel was able to recognize that God was calling out to him.

Have you ever experienced God calling out to you? In what ways does God call out to you every day? Record your experience below.

In what ways does having a relationship with God ground you in who you really are?

In the previous lesson, you read and reflected on passion. How do passion and calling intersect?

read The First Call

From *The Testament* by John Grisham[1]

He heard the guitar again. He opened his eyes and wiped his cheeks. Instead of seeing the young man in the pulpit, Nate saw the face of Christ, in agony and pain, dying on the cross. Dying for him.

A voice was calling Nate, a voice from within, a voice leading him down the aisle. But the invitation was confusing. He felt many conflicting emotions. His eyes were suddenly dry.

Why am I crying in a small hot chapel, listening to music I don't understand, in a town I'll never see again? The questions poured forth, the answers elusive.

It was one thing for God to forgive his astounding array of iniquities, and Nate certainly felt as though his burdens were lighter. But it was a far more difficult step to expect himself to become a follower.

As he listened to the music, he became bewildered. God couldn't be calling him. He was Nate O'Riley—boozer, addict, lover of women, absent father, miserable husband, greedy lawyer, swindler of tax money. The sad list went on and on.

He was dizzy. The music stopped and the young man prepared for another song. Nate hurriedly left the chapel. As he turned the corner, he glanced back, hoping to see Rachel, but also to make sure God hadn't sent someone to follow him.

first thoughts

like:

dislike:

agree:

disagree:

don't get it:

think

- Have you ever felt like Nate—that you were being called by God to do something but were afraid or unable to respond?
- When did God begin calling you? What did the calling sound like?
- What makes the difference between a person who responds to God's call and a person who runs from it?
- How persistent has God's calling been in your own life?

pray

read The Rebellious Prophet

Jonah 1:1-17

One day long ago, GOD's Word came to Jonah, Amittai's son: "Up on your feet and on your way to the big city of Nineveh! Preach to them. They're in a bad way and I can't ignore it any longer."

But Jonah got up and went the other direction to Tarshish, running away from God. He went down to the port of Joppa and found a ship headed for Tarshish. He paid the fare and went on board, joining those going to Tarshish — as far away from God as he could get.

But God sent a huge storm at sea, the waves towering.

The ship was about to break into pieces. The sailors were terrified. They called out in desperation to their gods. They threw everything they were carrying overboard to lighten the ship. Meanwhile, Jonah had gone down into the hold of the ship to take a nap. He was sound asleep. The captain came to him and said, "What's this? Sleeping! Get up! Pray to your god! Maybe your god will see we're in trouble and rescue us."

Then the sailors said to one another, "Let's get to the bottom of this. Let's draw straws to identify the culprit on this ship who's responsible for this disaster."

So they drew straws. Jonah got the short straw.

Then they grilled him: "Confess. Why this disaster? What is your work? Where do you come from? What country? What family?"

He told them, "I'm a Hebrew. I worship God, the God of heaven who made sea and land."

At that, the men were frightened, really frightened, and said, "What on earth have you done!" As Jonah talked, the sailors realized that he was running away from God.

They said to him, "What are we going to do with you — to get rid of this storm?" By this time the sea was wild, totally out of control.

Jonah said, "Throw me overboard, into the sea. Then the storm will stop. It's all my fault. I'm the cause of the storm. Get rid of me and you'll get rid of the storm."

But no. The men tried rowing back to shore. They made no headway. The storm only got worse and worse, wild and raging.

Then they prayed to God, "O God! Don't let us drown because of this man's life, and don't blame us for his death. You are God. Do what you think is best."

They took Jonah and threw him overboard. Immediately the sea was quieted down.

The sailors were impressed, no longer terrified by the sea, but in awe of God. They worshiped God, offered a sacrifice, and made vows.

Then God assigned a huge fish to swallow Jonah. Jonah was in the fish's belly three days and nights.

first thoughts

like:

dislike:

agree:

disagree:

don't get it:

think

- Have you ever felt, like Jonah, that God was calling you to do something you didn't want to do? Or something that was particularly difficult? Describe those situations.
- Is it possible to miss your calling? To what lengths will God go to help a person fulfill a calling?
- Read the rest of Jonah to consider how his identity and calling were related. Why would God use someone who seemingly

didn't want to see the people of Nineveh saved to present the message that would lead them to be saved? Do you see conflict between your desires and God's desire for you? How do you deal with that?

- How is your calling related to your true identity?

pray

read Choosing to Respond

From "Life Is Short" by Michelle Shortencarrier[3]

I debate which path I'll take to the Metro. I can go straight and pass the man waving his paper cup, calling out "nickels and quarters." Or I can go through the park where the men eat food from the white, beaten-up van. The eating men remind me of babies drinking their mothers' milk. I want to go through the park. I want to feel their humanness and witness their existence. I want to acknowledge they were born and will die. I want to love them. But I go straight. The nickel-and-quarter man is much easier to ignore.

first thoughts
like:
dislike:
agree:
disagree:
don't get it:

think

- How often do you face choices like the one described in this excerpt?
- Is it possible to ignore a calling? Have you ever tried to ignore the calling on your life?
- Why does God want us to identify with those we serve?
- Do you think life would be easier or more difficult without free will? Which would you choose? Why?

pray

read Highest Calling

Philippians 2:12-16

What I'm getting at, friends, is that you should simply keep on doing what you've done from the beginning. When I was living among you, you lived in responsive obedience. Now that I'm separated from you, keep it up. Better yet, redouble your efforts. Be energetic in your life of salvation, reverent and sensitive before God. That energy is *God's* energy, an energy deep within you, God himself willing and working at what will give him the most pleasure.

Do everything readily and cheerfully—no bickering, no second-guessing allowed! Go out into the world uncorrupted, a breath of fresh air in this squalid and polluted society. Provide people with a glimpse of good living and of the living God. Carry the light-giving Message into the night so I'll have good cause to be proud of you on the day that Christ returns. You'll be living proof that I didn't go to all this work for nothing.

---

first thoughts

like:

dislike:

agree:

disagree:

don't get it:

---

think

- What is the calling Paul describes that rests on the life of every believer?
- In what ways do you have the opportunity to demonstrate God to others?
- How bright is the light that shines on you? How bright is the light that shines in you?
- How does living as a "breath of fresh air" affect your identity?

pray

read The Weight of Calling

Acts 17:24-29

The God who made the world and everything in it, this Master of sky and land, doesn't live in custom-made shrines or need the human race to run errands for him, as if he couldn't take care of himself. He makes the creatures; the creatures don't make him. Starting from scratch, he made the entire human race and made the earth hospitable, with plenty of time and space for living so we could seek after God, and not just grope around in the dark but actually *find* him. He doesn't play hide-and-seek with us. He's not remote; he's *near*. We live and move in him, can't get away from him! One of your poets said it well: "We're the God-created." Well, if we are the God-created, it doesn't make a lot of sense to think we could hire a sculptor to chisel a god out of stone for *us*, does it?

---

first thoughts

like:

dislike:

agree:

disagree:

don't get it:

---

think

- If God can do everything Himself, why does He call people to do anything at all?
- Do you ever feel a weight from the calling you have on your life?
- How heavy is your calling? Does a weighty calling mean that you are not allowing God to bear enough of the weight?
- If your true identity is in Christ, how does that affect your response to a calling that seems burdensome?

pray

live The Redefining

Take a few moments to skim through the notes you've made in these readings. What do they tell you about your calling and how that intersects with your identity? Based on what you've read and discussed, is there anything you want to change? Describe this below.

What, if anything, is stopping you from making this change?

Do you feel that God has even given you a calling? In what ways is it your responsibility to make things happen in relation to your calling, and in what ways is it God's responsibility?

Do you think God gives people callings without giving them the desire and strength to fulfill the callings? Why or why not?

Talk with a close friend about all of the above. Brainstorm together about what it might take to move toward God in this area of your life. Determine what this looks like in a practical sense and then list any measurable goals you want to shoot for here. Review these goals each week to see how you're doing.

facing
failure

We believe that God hears our prayers. We
believe that he has the power to prevent bad
things (or losses). We believe that he always
acts in our best interest. Then why do we
respond so differently to defeats than we do
to victories?

John W. Samples

a reminder

Before you dive into this study, spend a little time reviewing what you wrote in the previous lessons' Live sections. How are you doing? Check with your small-group members and review your progress toward the specified goals. If necessary, adjust your goals and plans and then recommit to them.

the defining line

Failure has a way of stripping you of everything that says, "Things are just fine." It causes you to look closely at yourself. It reveals the foundation of who you are. It uncovers weaknesses, assumptions, and beliefs that you may not have even known you had. When was the last time you felt you had failed? Was it a few years ago? A few months ago? Or more recently? In the following space, create a working definition of failure.

Some people would argue that failure doesn't really exist—it's just a mere bump in the road to learning, growing, or doing something new. Do you think failure is real? Why or why not?

Think back to a time in your life when you felt like a failure. What about the circumstances made you feel like a failure? Consider sharing this with your group.

read Did Jesus Look Like a Failure?

Acts 2:22-28

Fellow Israelites, listen carefully to these words: Jesus the Nazarene, a man thoroughly accredited by God to you—the miracles and wonders and signs that God did through him are common knowledge—this Jesus, following the deliberate and well-thought-out plan of God, was betrayed by men who took the law into their own hands, and was handed over to you. And you pinned him to a cross and killed him. But God untied the death ropes and raised him up. Death was no match for him. David said it all:

> I saw God before me for all time.
>> Nothing can shake me; he's right by my side.
> I'm glad from the inside out, ecstatic;
>> I've pitched my tent in the land of hope.
> I know you'll never dump me in Hades;
>> I'll never even smell the stench of death.
> You've got my feet on the life-path,
>> with your face shining sun-joy all around.

---

first thoughts

like:

dislike:

agree:

disagree:

don't get it:

---

think

- How do you think Jesus' disciples initially reacted to His death on the cross? Do you think they wondered—even just for a moment—if Jesus had failed in His mission?
- How does God view failure?
- Why do you think God allows failure?
- In what ways can failure be part of God's redemptive plan?
- If failure is an invitation to run toward God, why is it so much easier to run away?

pray

read Facing Failure

From "Facing Failure" by Verla Gillmor[1]

As I handed my carefully wrapped package to the postal clerk, I thought, *By tomorrow, my publisher will have my manuscript, and in a few months I'll see a lifelong dream fulfilled—a published book!*

I expected to feel elated, but instead felt numb. Completing the project had been a mental, physical, emotional, and spiritual marathon. I felt as though every intelligent thought I'd ever had, I'd poured into that book. I didn't have a single word left in my brain!

A few days later, my editor called. "We love the manuscript. Just one more thing . . . we want you to write four more chapters. Get it to us as soon as possible. We're on a tight schedule."

It was as though I'd undergone a 9-month pregnancy, endured 24 hours of hard labor, delivered a beautiful baby, and a week later the obstetrician said, "You need to go back into labor for another 6 hours."

For the next three weeks, I struggled. I negotiated with God. I cried. Day after day, whatever I wrote went immediately into the wastebasket. Panic seeped into my thinking: I'm this close to the finish line, and I can't make it come together! The only thing that appeared certain was failure.

My extra book chapters eventually sprang to life—which is why I feel safer talking about them than a failed relationship or a failed business venture. Failure's something

first thoughts
like:
dislike:
agree:
disagree:
don't get it:

we'd rather talk about after it's overcome with subsequent success.

That's unfortunate, because failure teaches us things we can't learn any other way. The key is to treat failure as a visitor: allowed to deliver unpleasant news, but not allowed to take up permanent residence. We need to say, "Make your point—then leave."

Are you learning from your failures?

think

- What personal experiences with failure came to mind as you read this article excerpt?
- How is God's perspective about a failure in your life different from your own?
- What kind of impact has the fear of failure had on your life?
- What lessons has failure taught you about yourself? About God?
- How can you move beyond failure more swiftly?

pray

read Is It Possible to Fail God?

Psalm 51:1-6
A David psalm, after he was confronted by Nathan about the affair with Bathsheba.

Generous in love—God, give grace!
    Huge in mercy—wipe out my bad record.
Scrub away my guilt,
    soak out my sins in your laundry.
I know how bad I've been;
    my sins are staring me down.

You're the One I've violated, and you've seen
    it all, seen the full extent of my evil.
You have all the facts before you;
    whatever you decide about me is fair.
I've been out of step with you for a long time,
    in the wrong since before I was born.
What you're after is truth from the inside out.
    Enter me, then; conceive a new, true life.

---

first thoughts

like:

dislike:

agree:

disagree:

don't get it:

---

think

- In what ways does sin make you feel like you failed God?
- David has been called a "man after God's own heart." How do you reconcile that with the failures he clearly experienced? Does this offer you hope in your relationship with God? Explain.
- Is it possible to accept yourself for who you really are if you can't accept God's forgiveness? Is it possible to accept yourself for who you really are if you can't forgive yourself?

pray

read Embracing Failures

Isaiah 55:8-11

"I don't think the way you think.
     The way you work isn't the way I work."
          GOD's Decree.
"For as the sky soars high above earth,
     so the way I work surpasses the way you work,
     and the way I think is beyond the way you think.
Just as rain and snow descend from the skies
     and don't go back until they've watered the earth,
Doing their work of making things grow and blossom,
     producing seed for farmers and food for the hungry,
So will the words that come out of my mouth
     not come back empty-handed.
They'll do the work I sent them to do,
     they'll complete the assignment I gave them."

---

first thoughts

like:

dislike:

agree:

disagree:

don't get it:

---

think

- Can you provide an example from your own life that demonstrates how "the way you work isn't the way [God] work[s]"?
- How does God redeem failure? Are there any failures that are beyond His redemption? Explain.
- Who do you run to first when you face failure?
- Is your tendency to turn inward, to others, or to God for comfort? Why do you choose this response? What does it look like to turn to God for comfort when you've failed?

pray

read Transformation Through Brokenness

From "A Generation's Identity Crisis" by Adam Omelianchuk[2]

I remember sitting alongside the Mississippi River in St. Paul a couple of years ago as a broken man. I was so angry with God; I refused to speak to Him. I just sat there, smoking my tobacco pipe, listening to the flowing water for hours at a time. The only distractions were the occasional barge that would chug by and the twig I would sometimes dig in the dirt with. It was in these quiet moments that I was able to hear God speak to me. I would open my Bible to Isaiah 46 and read about the heavy idols I was carrying and how God longed for me to turn from my own self-glorification. Sometimes during my daily twaddle, I look back fondly on that time in my life. It was a turning point—a point of change. It was a change that I could not have done without, and neither can we. We must listen, or we will be nothing new under the sun.

---

first thoughts

like:

dislike:

agree:

disagree:

don't get it:

---

think

- Do you ever blame God for a failure you encountered?
- Are you honest and open with God about any anger you feel toward Him? What prevents you from being more honest?
- How can you make the most of failure? How can it become a "turning point" in your life?
- What is the greatest lesson you've learned from a difficult time? How has that shaped you?

pray

live   The Redefining

Take a few moments to skim through the notes you've made in these readings. What do they tell you about how you respond to failure? Based on what you've read and discussed, is there anything you want to change? Describe this below.

What, if anything, is stopping you from making this change?

How is failure an inhibitor in your life? Is there anything it's preventing you from doing right now?

Make a list of the top five failures you've experienced. How did those failures impact you as an individual? Share at least two of your failures with the members of your small group.

Talk with a close friend about all of the above. Brainstorm together about what it might take to move toward God in this area of your life. Determine what this looks like in a practical sense and then list any measurable goals you want to shoot for here. Review these goals each week to see how you're doing.

living the
God-infused
life

Has it ever occurred to you that one hundred pianos all tuned to the same fork are automatically tuned to each other? They are of one accord by being tuned, not to each other, but to another standard to which each one must individually bow. So one hundred worshippers meeting together, each one looking away to Christ, are in heart nearer to each other than they could possibly be were they to become "unity" conscious and turn their eyes away from God to strive for closer fellowship. Social religion is perfected when private religion is purified. The body becomes stronger as its members become healthier. The whole church of God gains when the members that compose it begin to seek a better and a higher life.

A. W. Tozer

a reminder

Before you dive into this study, spend a little time reviewing what you wrote in the previous lessons' Live sections. How are you doing? Check with your small-group members and review your progress toward the specified goals. If necessary, adjust your goals and plans and then recommit to them.

the defining line

Once you begin the active journey of knowing who you are and basing that foundation on the truths of God's Word, you can't help but begin to live the God-infused life. You can walk by the marketers, advertisers, and industries, knowing the truth. Will you completely avoid their influence? Probably not. But you will begin to realize and live out the truth that your value isn't enhanced by anything you buy on this earth. And your value isn't made greater by what you do—you're already seen as priceless in the eyes of the One who made you.

Think back on all of the previous lessons in this discussion guide. What have you learned about your identity that can help you live the God-infused life?

What stops you from allowing God to infuse all of your life? What parts of yourself—your identity—are you still trying to hold back from Him?

read Real Life

Colossians 3:3-17

Your old life is dead. Your new life, which is your *real* life—even though invisible to spectators—is with Christ in God. *He* is your life. When Christ (your real life, remember) shows up again on this earth, you'll show up, too—the real you, the glorious you. Meanwhile, be content with obscurity, like Christ.

And that means killing off everything connected with that way of death: sexual promiscuity, impurity, lust, doing whatever you feel like whenever you feel like it, and grabbing whatever attracts your fancy. That's a life shaped by things and feelings instead of by God. It's because of this kind of thing that God is about to explode in anger. It wasn't long ago that you were doing all that stuff and not knowing any better. But you know better now, so make sure it's all gone for good: bad temper, irritability, meanness, profanity, dirty talk.

Don't lie to one another. You're done with that old life. It's like a filthy set of ill-fitting clothes you've stripped off and put in the fire. Now you're dressed in a new wardrobe. Every item of your new way of life is custom-made by the Creator, with his label on it. All the old fashions are now obsolete. Words like Jewish and non-Jewish, religious and irreligious, insider and outsider, uncivilized and uncouth, slave and free, mean nothing. From now on everyone is defined by Christ, everyone is included in Christ.

So, chosen by God for this new life of love, dress in the wardrobe God picked out for you: compassion, kindness, humility,

first thoughts

like:

dislike:

agree:

disagree:

don't get it:

quiet strength, discipline. Be even-tempered, content with second place, quick to forgive an offense. Forgive as quickly and completely as the Master forgave you. And regardless of what else you put on, wear love. It's your basic, all-purpose garment. Never be without it.

Let the peace of Christ keep you in tune with each other, in step with each other. None of this going off and doing your own thing. And cultivate thankfulness. Let the Word of Christ—the Message—have the run of the house. Give it plenty of room in your lives. Instruct and direct one another using good common sense. And sing, sing your hearts out to God! Let every detail in your lives—words, actions, whatever—be done in the name of the Master, Jesus, thanking God the Father every step of the way.

think

- What does Paul mean when he writes, "From now on everyone is defined by Christ, everyone is included in Christ"? How does that truth impact you personally?
- What does a God-infused lifestyle look like?
- What are the greatest obstacles to living as described in the passage above?
- Is Paul's description of a God-infused lifestyle a realistic goal or an unrealistic ideal?
- How does this description match with what you perceive is your true identity?

pray

read A Moment of Reflection

Isaiah 46:8-11

"Think about this. Wrap your minds around it.
    This is serious business, rebels. Take it to heart.
Remember your history,
    your long and rich history.
I am GOD, the only God you've had or ever will have—
    incomparable, irreplaceable—
From the very beginning
    telling you what the ending will be,
All along letting you in
    on what is going to happen,
Assuring you, 'I'm in this for the long haul,
    I'll do exactly what I set out to do,'
Calling that eagle, Cyrus, out of the east,
    from a far country the man I chose to help me.
I've said it, and I'll most certainly do it.
    I've planned it, so it's as good as done."

---

first thoughts

like:

dislike:

agree:

disagree:

don't get it:

---

think

- Reflecting on your own past, how have you seen God prove Himself true in your life?
- Using everyday language, describe God's faithfulness to you.
- What can you actively do to remind yourself that you're not alone, even when you feel alone?
- In what ways does God's constant presence enable you to live the God-infused life?

pray

read Beyond the Rumors

Job 42:1-6

Job answered GOD:
"I'm convinced: You can do anything and everything.
    Nothing and no one can upset your plans.
You asked, 'Who is this muddying the water,
    ignorantly confusing the issue, second-guessing my purposes?'
I admit it. I was the one. I babbled on about things far beyond me,
    made small talk about wonders way over my head.
You told me, 'Listen, and let me do the talking.
    Let me ask the questions. *You* give the answers.'
I admit I once lived by rumors of you;
    now I have it all firsthand—from my own eyes and ears!
I'm sorry—forgive me. I'll never do that again, I promise!
    I'll never again live on crusts of hearsay, crumbs of rumor."

---

first thoughts

like:

dislike:

agree:

disagree:

don't get it:

---

think

- In what ways have you lived by "rumors of God"?
- Why is it often easier to second-guess God than to trust in His faithfulness?
- Describe areas in your life where you are currently second-guessing God. What will it take to move from second-guessing to trusting in His plans?
- How does knowing that God can do "anything and everything" affect your feelings about your future?

pray

read Built on an Eternal Foundation

2 Corinthians 5:1-14

We know that when these bodies of ours are taken down like tents and folded away, they will be replaced by resurrection bodies in heaven—God-made, not handmade—and we'll never have to relocate our "tents" again. Sometimes we can hardly wait to move—and so we cry out in frustration. Compared to what's coming, living conditions around here seem like a stopover in an unfurnished shack, and we're tired of it! We've been given a glimpse of the real thing, our true home, our resurrection bodies! The Spirit of God whets our appetite by giving us a taste of what's ahead. He puts a little of heaven in our hearts so that we'll never settle for less.

That's why we live with such good cheer. You won't see us drooping our heads or dragging our feet! Cramped conditions here don't get us down. They only remind us of the spacious living conditions ahead. It's what we trust in but don't yet see that keeps us going. Do you suppose a few ruts in the road or rocks in the path are going to stop us? When the time comes, we'll be plenty ready to exchange exile for homecoming.

But neither exile nor homecoming is the main thing. Cheerfully pleasing God is the main thing, and that's what we aim to do, regardless of our conditions. Sooner or later we'll all have to face God, regardless of our conditions. We will appear before Christ and take what's coming to us as a result of our actions, either good or bad.

That keeps us vigilant, you can be sure. It's no light thing to know that we'll all one day stand in that place of Judgment. That's why we work urgently with every-

first thoughts

like:

dislike:

agree:

disagree:

don't get it:

one we meet to get them ready to face God. God alone knows how well we do this, but I hope you realize how much and deeply we care. We're not saying this to make ourselves look good to you. We just thought it would make you feel good, proud even, that we're on your side and not just nice to your face as so many people are. If I acted crazy, I did it for God; if I acted overly serious, I did it for you. Christ's love has moved me to such extremes. His love has the first and last word in everything we do.

Our firm decision is to work from this focused center: One man died for everyone. That puts everyone in the same boat.

think

- In what ways do you feel you have "heaven in your heart"?
- What kind of everyday impact is there to knowing you are built on an eternal foundation?
- Do you feel ready to "face God"? Why or why not?
- How does Christ's love move you? How does it affect who you are?

pray

read Steadfast in His Permanent Love

Ephesians 1:3-14

How blessed is God! And what a blessing he is! He's the Father of our Master, Jesus Christ, and takes us to the high places of blessing in him. Long before he laid down earth's foundations, he had us in mind, had settled on us as the focus of his love, to be made whole and holy by his love. Long, long ago he decided to adopt us into his family through Jesus Christ. (What pleasure he took in planning this!) He wanted us to enter into the celebration of his lavish gift-giving by the hand of his beloved Son.

Because of the sacrifice of the Messiah, his blood poured out on the altar of the Cross, we're a free people—free of penalties and punishments chalked up by all our misdeeds. And not just barely free, either. Abundantly free! He thought of everything, provided for everything we could possibly need, letting us in on the plans he took such delight in making. He set it all out before us in Christ, a long-range plan in which everything would be brought together and summed up in him, everything in deepest heaven, everything on planet earth.

It's in Christ that we find out who we are and what we are living for. Long before we first heard of Christ and got our hopes up, he had his eye on us, had designs on us for glorious living, part of the overall purpose he is working out in everything and everyone.

It's in Christ that you, once you heard the truth and believed it (this Message of your salvation), found yourselves home free—signed, sealed, and delivered by the Holy Spirit. This signet

---

first thoughts

like:

dislike:

agree:

disagree:

don't get it:

---

from God is the first installment on what's coming, a reminder that we'll get everything God has planned for us, a praising and glorious life.

think

- What does it mean to you to be "abundantly free"? How does that impact how you see yourself?
- Make a list of all the things this passage says about who you are in Christ. Which of those things did you need to hear the most today?
- Which of the things on the list are the most surprising to you? Which of the things on the list are you still trying to do or accomplish on your own?
- Which of the things on the list are dependent on you? What does that look like? What does that require of you?

pray

live   The Redefining

Take a few moments to skim through the notes you've made in these readings. What do they tell you about living the God-infused life? Based on what you've read and discussed, is there anything you want to change? Describe it below.

What, if anything, is stopping you from making this change?

Is there anything in your life—compromise, sin, doubt, anger—that is preventing you from going deeper in your relationship with God? If so, spend some time this week talking to God about this.

Jesus instructs us to "love others as well as you love yourself" (Matthew 22:39). In what ways have you failed to love yourself? How can knowing your true identity in Christ help to change that?

Talk with a close friend about all of the above. Brainstorm together about what it might take to move toward God in this area of your life. Determine what this looks like in a practical sense and then list any measurable goals you want to shoot for.

Even though you've reached the end of the discussion guide, the progress toward a better understanding of identity continues. Commit to discussing your goals and discoveries with small-group members or friends as you attempt to live a God-infused life every day.

discussion group
study tips

After going through the study on your own, it's time to sit down with others and go deeper. A group of eight to ten is optimal, but smaller groups will allow members to participate more. Here are a few thoughts on how to make the most of your group discussion time.

Set ground rules. You don't need many. Here are two:

First, you'll want group members to make a commitment to the entire eight-week study. A binding legal document with notarized signatures and commitments written in blood probably isn't necessary—but you know your friends best. Just remember this: Significant personal growth happens when group members spend enough time together to really get to know each other. Hit-and-miss attendance rarely allows this to occur.

Second, agree together that everyone's story is important. Time is a valuable commodity, so if you have only an hour to spend together, do your best to give each person ample time to express concerns, pass along insights, and generally feel like a participating member of the group. Small-group discussions are not monologues.

Meet regularly. Choose a time and place and stick to it. No one likes showing up to a restaurant at noon, only to discover that the meeting was moved to seven in the evening at so-and-so's house. Consistency removes stress that could otherwise frustrate discussion and subsequent personal growth. It's only eight weeks. You can do this.

Think ahead. Whoever is leading or organizing the study needs to keep an eye on the calendar. No matter what day or time you pick, you're probably going to run into a date that just doesn't work for people. Maybe it's a holiday. Maybe there's a huge concert or conference in town. Maybe there's a random week when everyone is going to be out of town. Keep in communication with each other about the meetings and be flexible if you do have to reschedule a meeting or skip a week.

Talk openly. If you enter this study with shields up, you're probably not alone. And you're not a "bad person" for your hesitation to unpack your life in front of friends or strangers. Maybe you're skeptical about the value of revealing the deepest parts of who you are to others. Maybe you're simply too afraid of what might fall out of the suitcase. You don't have to go to a place where you're uncomfortable. If you want to sit and listen, offer a few thoughts, or even express a surface level of your own pain, go ahead. But don't neglect what brings you to this place—that desperation. You can't ignore it away. Dip your feet in the water of brutally honest discussion and you may choose to dive in. There is healing here.

Stay on task. Be wary of sharing material that falls into the Too Much Information (TMI) category. Don't spill unnecessary stuff. This is about discovering how *you* can be a better person.

Hold each other accountable. The Live section is an important gear in the "redefinition" machine. If you're really ready for positive change—for spiritual growth—you'll want to take this section seriously. Get personal when you summarize your discoveries. Be practical as you compose your goals. And make sure you're realistic as you determine a plan for accountability. Be extraordinarily loving but brutally honest as you examine each other's Live sections. The stuff on this page must be doable. Don't hold back—this is where the rubber meets the road.

frequently asked questions

I'm stuck. I've read the words on the page, but they just don't connect. Am I missing something?

Be patient. There's no need for speed-reading. Reread the words. Pray about them. Reflect on the questions at the bottom of the page. Consider rewriting the reading in a way that makes sense to you. Meditate on one idea at a time. Read Scripture passages in different Bible translations. Ask a friend for help. Skip the section and come back to it later. And don't beat yourself up if you still don't connect. Turn the page and keep seeking.

This study includes a wide variety of readings. Some are intended to provoke. Others are intended to subdue. Some are meant to apply to a thinker, others to a feeler, and still others to an experiential learner. If your groove is pop culture, science, relationships, art, or something completely different, there's something in here that you're naturally going to click with, but that doesn't mean that you should just brush off the rest of the readings. It means that in those no-instant-click moments, you're going to have to broaden your perspective and think outside your own box. You may be surprised by what you discover.

One or two people in our small group tend to dominate the discussion. Is there any polite way of handling this?

Did you set up ground rules with your group? If not, review the suggestions above and incorporate them. Then do this: Before each discussion, remind participants that each person's thoughts, insights, concerns, and opinions are important. Note the time you have for your meeting and then dive in.

If this still doesn't help, you may need to speak to the person who has arm-wrestled control. Do so in a loving manner, expressing your sincere concern for what the person is talking about and inviting others to weigh in as well. Please note: A one-person-dominated discussion isn't always a bad thing. Your role in a small group is not only to explore and expand your own understanding; it's also to support one another. If someone truly needs more of the floor, give it to him. There will be times when the needs of the one outweigh the needs of the many. Use good judgment and allow extra space when needed. Your time might be next week.

One or two people in our small group rarely say anything. How should we handle this?

Recognize that not everyone will be comfortable sharing. Depending on her background, personality, and comfort level, an individual may rarely say anything at all. There are two things to remember. First, love a person right where she is. This may be one of her first experiences as part of a Bible discussion group. She may be feeling insecure because she doesn't know the Bible as well as other members of the group. She may just be shy or introverted. She may still be sorting out what she believes. Whatever the case, make her feel welcome and loved. Thank her for coming, and if she misses a meeting, call to check up on her. After one of the studies, you may want to ask her what she thought about the discussion. And after a few meetings, you can try to involve her in the discussion by asking everyone in the group to respond to a certain question. Just make sure the question you ask doesn't put anyone on the spot.

During our meeting time, we find ourselves spending so much time catching up with each other — what happened over the previous week — that we don't have enough time for the actual study.

If the friendships within your group grow tight, you may need to establish some time just to hang out and catch up with one another. This is a healthy part of a successful discussion group. You can do this before or after the actual study group time. Some groups prefer to share a meal together before the actual study, and other groups prefer to stay afterward and munch on snacks. Whatever your group chooses, it's important to have established start and finish times for your group members. That way, the people who are on a tight schedule can know when to show up to catch the main part of the meeting.

At our meetings, there are times when one or two people will become really vulnerable about something they're struggling with or facing. It's an awkward thing for our group to try to handle. What should we do?

This study is designed to encourage group members to get real and be vulnerable. But how your group deals with those vulnerabilities will determine how much deeper your group can go. If a person is sharing something that makes him particularly vulnerable, avoid offering a quick, fix-it answer. Even if you know how to heal deep hurts, cure eating disorders, or overcome depression in one quick answer, hold your tongue. Most people who make themselves vulnerable aren't looking for a quick fix. They want two things: to know they aren't alone and to be supported. If you can identify with their hurt, say so, without one-upping their story with your own. Second, let the person know you'll pray for him, and if the moment is right, go ahead and pray for him right then. If the moment isn't right, then you may want to pray for him at the end of the meeting. Walking through these vulnerable times is tricky business, and it's going to take a lot of prayer and listening to God's leading to get you through.

Some group members don't prepare before our meetings. How can we encourage them to read ahead of time?

It can be frustrating, particularly as a leader, when group members don't read the material; but don't let this discourage you. You can begin each lesson by reading the section together as a group so that everyone is on the same page. And you can gently encourage group members to read during the week. But ultimately, what really matters is that they show up and are growing spiritually alongside you. The REDEFINING LIFE studies aren't about homework; they're about personal spiritual growth, and that takes place in many ways—both inside and outside this book. So if someone's slacking on the outside, it's okay. You have no idea how much she may be growing or being challenged on the inside.

Our group members are having a tough time reaching their goals. What can we do?

First of all, review the goals you've set. Are they realistic? How would you measure a goal of "don't be frustrated at work"? Rewrite the goals until they're bite-sized and reasonable—and reachable. How about "Take an online personality test" or "Make a list of what's good and what's not-so-good about my career choices so I can talk about it with discussion group members" or "Start keeping a prayer journal." Get practical. Get real. And don't forget to marinate everything in lots of prayer.

notes

Lesson 1

1. Frederica Matthewes-Green, "A Clear and Present Identity," *Christianity Today*, September 4, 2000, www.christianitytoday.com.
2. "Take Five with Kurt Warner," *Today's Christian Woman*, January/February 2003, 14.
3. "Misfit," *Vanity Fair*, April 1998, 98.

Lesson 2

1. Susan Horsburgh and Steve Barnes, "Born Again," *People*, July 28, 2003, 53–54.
2. Kenneth J. Gergen, "The Decline and Fall of Personality," *Psychology Today*, November 1992.

Lesson 3

1. Caleb C. Anderson, "Who I'm Not," *Relevant*, March 9, 2004, www.relevantmagazine.com.
2. John Mackey, quoted in Charles Fishman, "The Anarchist's Cookbook," *Fast Company*, July 2004, 70.

Lesson 4

1. Frank Darabont, *The Shawshank Redemption*, screenplay based on the short story "Rita Hayworth and Shawshank Redemption" by Stephen King, 1994, Castle Rock Pictures.
2. From *The Hitchhiker's Guide to the Galaxy* by Douglas Adams, copyright © 1979 by Douglas Adams. Used by permission of Harmony Books, a division of Random House, Inc., 177–182.

Lesson 5

1. Lynne Truss, *Eats, Shoots & Leaves: The Zero Tolerance Approach to Punctuation* (New York: Gotham Books, 2004), pp. xxi-xxiii.

2. From an interview in *Biography Magazine*, February 2003, 42, 44.

3. *Newsweek*, November 24, 2003, 62.

4. J. L. Eubanks, "I Know Passion," *Relevant*, n.d., www.relevantmagazine.com.

Lesson 6

1. John Grisham, *The Testament* (New York: Doubleday, 1999), 306–307.

2. Michelle Shortencarrier, "Life Is Short," *Washington Post*, August 15, 2004, D1.

Lesson 7

1. Verla Gillmor, "Facing Failure," *Today's Christian Woman*, May/June 2001, 66.

2. Adam Omelianchuk, "A Generation's Identity Crisis," *Relevant*, January 26, 2004, http://www.relevantmagazine.com/article.php?sid=2610.

OWN YOUR FAITH.